Everlasting Flowers

Everlasting Flowers

Patricia Crosher

B.T. Batsford Ltd · London

Acknowledgements

Very special thanks go to my daughter, Philippa Whitaker, for word processing my manuscript and for being so wonderfully patient, and to her husband, John, for his valuable help. Thanks also go to my other daughter, Penelope Kalli, for her advice and encouragement and to my husband, Tom, for his faith and constructive criticism. Last, but by no means least, I would like to thank my exceptionally talented photographer, Ian Wren, for his meticulous care and understanding.

First published 1996

© Patricia Crosher 1996
Photography by Ian Wren
13 Dove Rise, Oadby, Leicester
Cover photograph by Andrew Cameron

Designed and typeset by Peter Higgins
Printed in Hong Kong

Published by
B.T. Batsford Ltd
4 Fitzhardinge Street
London W1H 0AH

A catalogue record for this book is available from the British Library

ISBN 0 7134 7533 1

contents

drying, preserving & artificial materials

equipment & techniques

arrangements

introduction

Artificial flowers and fruits can be so realistic and, with a little imagination and some basic skills, they can be used to make beautiful arrangements. I hope the guidelines, tips and ideas in this book will inspire and enthuse you to experiment with the wealth of artificial materials available and to create your own designs.

Combining dried and glycerined foliage with silk flowers produces excellent results. Creating the perfect arrangement is basically a matter of making a harmonious choice of suitable elements and occasionally adding ribbons from the complementary range which is now widely available. When your final arrangement is complete and you are satisfied with the result, the sense of achievement is reward in itself.

When you are out in the country or at the beach, take the opportunity to look for interesting components for future use in an arrangement. Stones, seedpods and pieces of driftwood for example should all attract your attention. Your perceptions will, of course, be heightened, as your observations would be if you were tackling a drawing or painting. You will notice that the individual flowers face in different ways on the same plant, that the leaves are different shapes and sizes, that grey leaves go with pink flowers, bronze with red, bright and dark green with yellow and so on.

Sadly, time is always so scarce, particularly when it comes to buying and arranging fresh flowers. Artificial, dried and preserved arrangements provide a very attractive, cost-effective and long-lasting alternative. Of course, fresh materials do have a special beauty that can sometimes be difficult to match with artificial flowers and foliage. However, if you choose and style your materials well, you can create wonderful arrangements for the home or make lovely gifts for almost every occasion.

drying, preser
& artificial ma

ving
erials

plants for drying

If you are able to grow your own plants for drying, you are at an advantage. Different plants need to be gathered at certain times of the year – although April to September are usually the busiest months – and they should be treated immediately after picking so they retain a lovely fresh look. It is therefore extremely convenient if your raw materials are close at hand.

However, florists, nurseries and garden centres are becoming increasingly well stocked and, of course, wild areas are full of beautiful flowers and grasses. They must be picked at an appropriate time though and wild grasses, such as those shown in the photograph on page 15, must be gathered in spring. Always remember not to pick a protected or endangered species, and never pick a strip bare – make sure you leave plenty to seed. No matter whether you are using wild or cultivated material, the overall aim when it is dried is that it should retain its shape and colour. The photograph below shows some of my favourite standbys.

Below: A selection of useful and easily dried flowers, foliage and seedheads

The following list features plants which are most suitable for drying. It is by no means exhaustive.

Acanthus (bear's breeches)
Fairly large perennial plants with spiky leaves and flowers in dull shades of mauve, pink and cream growing around thick stems. Useful for large arrangements. Dries easily. Hang to dry.

Achillea 'Moonshine' (achillea/yarrow)
A hardy perennial plant with flowers made up of many small florets on woody stems. Does not need wiring. Pick when all the flowers are completely out but do not wait until they begin to turn brown. Hang to dry quickly. Never hang if at all damp.

Alchemilla mollis (lady's mantle)
This is a perennial plant with showy, lime-green, star-like flowers flowing in all directions over the stems. I could not do without this plant, finding it particularly useful for dainty or celebratory arrangements. Hang to dry, but note that it can be brittle when dried. It can also be glycerined (see page 21).

Ammobium alatum (sandflower)
A half-hardy annual with small, white, papery flowers with yellow centres, which are suitable for use in pictures. The stems are strong but do not always grow straight. Pick the flowers before they are fully out otherwise the centres turn brown. Some stems may need wiring. Hang to dry.

Anaphalis nubigena (pearl everlasting)
A hardy perennial plant with a grey stem and grey leaves. It has papery white flowers growing at the top. Suitable for arrangements, but I prefer to use it for pictures. Hang to dry.

Artemisia (artemisia)

Aromatic, perennial plant with fern-like grey foliage. The flowers are insignificant, so pick the stems at the end of the year when the plant is in bud. Mainly useful for delicate arrangements. Hang to dry.

Astilbe (astilbe)

A perennial that comes in a variety of colours from cream to dark red. Needs plenty of water in dry weather. Pick before fully out. Useful when spikes are needed. Hang to dry. Shrinks quite considerably when dried.

Astrantia (starwort)

Easily-grown perennial that spreads well. Flowers: pretty, delicate-looking, pale pink with a touch of green, and white with green. The flowers look dry on the plant. The more it is picked, the more it flowers. Dries very easily by hanging. There is also a variegated leaf plant.

Atriplex (red mountain spinach)

A. hortensis var. *rubra* is an annual plant which is very useful for lineage. When established in the garden, it seeds prolifically. Hang to dry.

Digitalis (foxglove)

A perennial plant with most attractive funnel-shaped flowers. It is easy to grow from seed. New colours have recently become available which look wonderful in fresh arrangements. However, the flowers are not really suitable for drying, although this may be possible with desiccants. The seedheads, picked when green, are easy to dry. They are useful for background material in large arrangements. Dry standing in a container.

Foxglove seedheads

Lavender

Lady's mantle and astilbe

Poppy seedheads

Echinops (globe thistle)

Thistle-like hardy perennial with globe flowers in white or blue. Pick when the flower is barely showing colour. Hang to dry.

Erica (heather)

Small evergreen bushes which flower in all seasons. Can be hung to dry but may drop if not gathered at the right time i.e. when they are just out. Finding the right drying method is a case of trial and error as the varieties are so numerous. Flowers range from white to pink and purple.

Eryngium (sea holly)

Similar to the globe thistle, but with smaller, more delicate, blue thistles on numerous blue stems. Its blue is more dominant than that of the globe thistle. Harvest when full of colour. If picking is delayed, it loses its colour. Hang to air dry.

Gypsophila (baby's breath)

A hardy perennial with delicate cream flowers. The double form of *G. elegens* is the best to buy as it is easier to dry than the other varieties. Hang bunches to dry.

Helichrysum bracteatum (strawflower)

Half-hardy annual which can be grown from seed. Very useful and popular. Available in a variety of colours. Gather on a fine day when completely free from any moisture. The first flowers on the plants are the biggest and prettiest. Cut these off leaving a small stem before they have fully opened and wire them individually, leaving the rest to grow larger. Can be bought ready dried but I prefer to dry my own. The flowers do continue to grow even after being wired and left to dry.

Helipterum manglesii (everlasting daisy)
Half-hardy annual. The silvery-pink buds are prettier than the open flowers, so pick when just showing pink or white – some will then open up. Hang to dry.

Herbs
Many herbs can be dried and it is worth trying a variety to see which can be used with most success. Mint, for example, has pretty mauve flowers; the variegated type has white ones. The tiny flowers grow half-way up the stems, culminating in a point. Most types of mint have a nice aroma and are useful for pot-pourri and for small arrangements. Mint, and most other herbs, need their flowers picked to prevent the plants going to seed. Hang to dry.

Hosta (hosta)
Useful for its attractive foliage. Dry the leaves by placing them in wet Oasis until the water has evaporated. (Photograph on page 18 shows a dried hosta leaf.)

Hydrangea (hydrangea)
Perennial plant usually started in a pot or bought to grow in the garden. After planting, a season often elapses before it flowers again. Can grow up to just under two metres (six feet) in height. The large round heads are made up of many flowers on woody stems. Pick when the flowers feel papery to the touch and before they turn brown, usually during the two months before the frosts start. Leave some on the bush or it may not flower the following year. Easy to dry if put in a little water and left until the water has evaporated. Avoid cutting back the bushes too much.

Iris foetidissima (stinking iris)
The flowers of this perennial plant are of no consequence although the seedheads and occasionally the leaves are useful. Hardly need to be

dried as they will be almost dry when gathered. The seeds inside the pods can be taken out and glued back in position or left out if unwanted.

Lavandula (lavender)
Fresh-smelling perennial with tiny flowers in light and dark blue, white, mauve or pink. An ideal flower for drying. Pick before the flowers are out and after a period of twenty four hours without rain. Must not be at all damp when hung to dry.

Liatris (blazing star)
Tall spikes with small, densely-packed pink and mauve flowers growing round the stem from top to bottom. Pick before the first flower dies, although as they remain in flower for some time, this can be difficult to judge. Extremely useful for large baskets. Hang to dry.

Limonium sinuatum (statice)
Half-hardy annual which can be grown from seed. Extremely popular in dried arrangements and available in a range of colours. Should be left to grow until every small floret is well open. Does not need wiring as the stems harden when dried. Hang to dry.

Moss
Useful types are bun moss (*Grimmia pulvinata*), reindeer moss (*Cladonia rangifernia*) and also sphagnum moss. Some types are imported and can be bought ready-dried from florists but you can gather fresh moss and dry in a warm place.

Narcissus (daffodil)
Numerous varieties. Although they do desiccate, they are a little difficult to keep – they last better under a glass dome.

Nigella (love-in-a-mist)
Delicate pink, white and blue flowers encased in

the original weeds. Hang to dry in the green stage; the mature seedheads are dry already.

Phlomis fruticosa (Jerusalem sage)
This is more a bush than a plant and has green-grey leaves and pale-yellow flowers arranged in whorls up square stems. The flowers are not worth drying. However, the green seedheads are attractive and do not take much drying.

Physalis franchetii (Chinese lantern)
This hardy perennial has swollen orange/yellow calyxes or pods, lantern-like in shape, which hang down from the stem. These are easily damaged so wire using thin wire and dry them on their own in an airing cupboard until stiff. This can be done at all stages from green to green/orange and then orange. Very attractive for fruit arrangements, swags and cones.

Protea (protea)
A shrub which has flowers with coloured bracts arranged in fancy heads. They are imported. The bud shown on the left was bought fresh and then dried. They keep their pinkish colour indefinitely.

Rosa (rose)
Perennial. Buds are best for successful drying. Pick them in their early stages and hang to dry; this is not an easy task, but a matter of trial and error. Desiccants are better for the flowers.

Rumex (dock)
Dock seedheads are a particularly lovely colour. Can be picked when green or pinkish, but if you wait until they have turned brown, they will eventually drop. Hang to dry.

Salix lanata (pussy willow)
Has a soft, felt-like texture and forms a wonderful colour combination with glycerined material.

green leaf spikes. Flowers will dry sometimes, and are also suitable for pressing. The seed-heads are quite lovely. Hang to dry.

From left to right:
Stinking iris; dock seed-heads; bear's breeches; protea bud; lamb's tongue; pussy willow

Papaver (poppy)
Perennial/annual. Poppies themselves are too delicate to dry, but the seedheads are a must. Colours include grey, blue, striped, brown and black. I pick them in the green stage and observe what colours they turn. I end up with thousands of seeds after drying. One year I put them round a hedgerow near my house; some of them germinated and flowered, looking much nicer than

Santolina (lavender cotton)

Small, grey-white leaves with flat, yellow button flowers. The flowers dry well and are most suitable for small arrangements. Hang to dry.

Sedum spectabile (ice plant)

The flat heads of the ice plant, particularly 'Autumn Joy', are useful for creating volume in an arrangement. Hang to dry at the end of the season.

Solidago (golden rod)

The tall yellow spikes of this perennial plant dry well if picked early enough; if picked too late they become fluffy when dried. Cut when beginning to flower and hang to dry, heads down.

Stachys lanata (lamb's tongue)

These plants have velvet-grey leaves and mauve flowers, but it is the grey seedheads which are the most useful. Do not use when wet. Hang the seedheads to dry.

Xeranthemum annuum (immortelle)

The star-shaped flowers on this hardy annual plant range from white and pink to purple. They flower in late-summer and continue till the frosts commence. Hang to air dry.

Zinnia (zinnia)

These annual/perennial plants, which need plenty of sun and dry weather, have lovely ball-shaped flowers with colourings in the orange and peach range. Cut when fully out but before the pollen is shed. Remove heads, and wire before drying in desiccants.

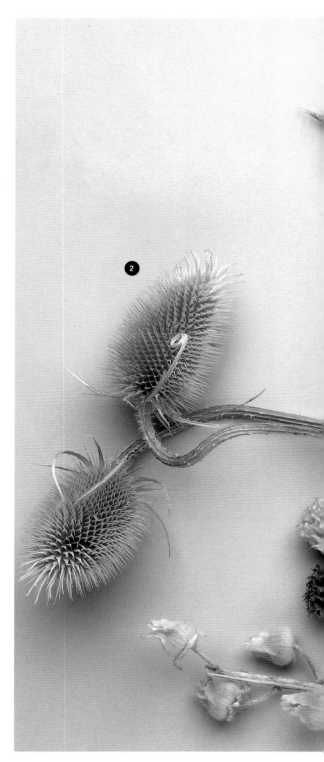

1. A collection of dried
   wild grasses, thistles
   and flowers

2. Teasles

3. Foxglove seedheads

4. Jerusalem sage seed-
   heads

drying & preserving

Always prepare plant material as follows before putting it away to dry.

Method

1. Cut stems at a slant, as this facilitates inserting them into Oasis.
2. With flowers, strip off all dead and untidy bits and pieces. This usually includes most leaves, especially those at the bottom of the stem and those which have been eaten or marked, as well as all the nodules on the stem. Don't cut the stems too short – they are useful for wiring.
3. Hang the material downwards, preferably tied in bunches, unless otherwise stated.

This allows the sap to circulate, keeping leaves and petals fresh until they have had time to dry thoroughly.

4. Do not leave materials to dry for too long – they should feel crisp to the touch when sufficiently dry.
5. Store surplus material in a box or basket with a lid, making sure the container has some air holes.
6. Black tissue paper is best for wrapping bunches.

There are several ways of preserving plant material. Experience will show you the method best suited to each type of plant.

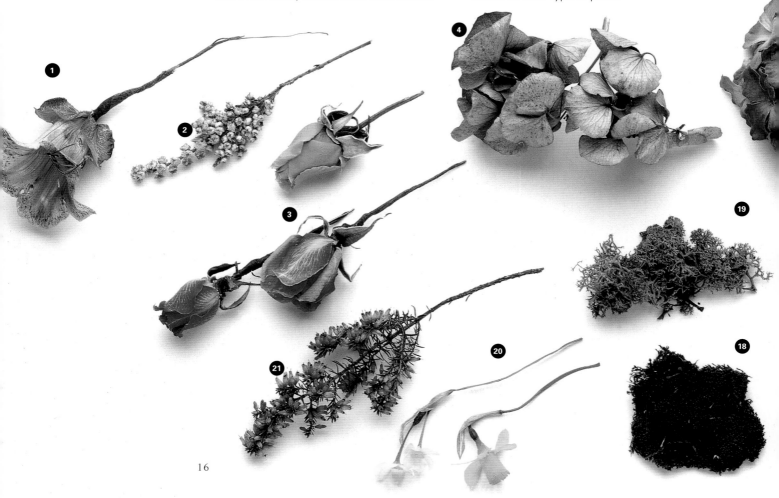

Air drying

With some exceptions (e.g. seed pods), material for air drying should be gathered well before its life cycle is over. It should be picked on a dry day, never immediately after rain, and preferably at noon when the sun is at its highest. After gathering, separate foliage and flowers and remove most of the leaves from flower stems. Then tie the material in bunches and hang it to dry with heads down in a dry, warm and preferably dark room. This speeds the drying process, ensuring a good colour.

Drying natural fruits, vegetables and large buds

When dried, natural fruits and vegetables make attractive additions to certain types of arrangement. They lend textural interest as well as rich colour.

Pomegranates, oak apples, lychees, aubergines, chillies, lemons and oranges can all be dried in the same way. Cocktail sticks can be used for the smaller items, slightly bigger sticks (such as wooden skewers) for the larger ones. Push the pointed end of the stick into the base

1. *Cobaea scandens*; desiccant-dried
2. Heather; desiccant-dried
3. Roses; desiccant-dried
4. Hydrangea florets; left standing in water to dry out
5. Silk hydrangea floret
6. Globe thistle; hung to dry
7. *Polygonum*; hung to dry
8. Immortelle; hung to dry
9. Thistle; hung to dry
10. Poppy bud; hung to dry
11. Golden rod; hung to dry
12. Chinese lantern seed pod; hung to dry
13. *Ajuga reptans*; hung to dry
14. Zinnia; desiccant-dried
15. Zinnia; desiccant-dried
16. Rose; hung to dry
17. Ivy berries; dried in a warm place
18. Reindeer moss; dried in a warm place
19. English moss; dried in a warm place
20. Miniature daffodils; desiccant-dried
21. Heather; desiccant-dried

1. Drying roses in a desiccant
2. Dried corn
3. Dried lemon
4. Magnolia bud
5. Horse chestnut
6. Dried avocado
7. Lychees
8. Dried chillies
9. Dried oak apple
10. Cocktail sticks
11. Dried pomegranate
12. Hosta leaf

of the material and place it on a tray in an airing cupboard. Insert two cocktail sticks or skewers for oranges and lemons. Turn the vegetable or piece of fruit at frequent intervals. When fully dry, it should feel quite light.

Chestnuts can be put straight into an airing cupboard to dry – they can look most attractive when polished or varnished. Pick magnolia buds only when there is an abundance of them and, again, these can be dried in an airing cupboard. Their velvet looks good against a shiny chestnut.

Desiccants

There are several types of desiccant which can be used for preserving plant material, particularly flowers. They work by absorbing the moisture contained within petals and leaves. Desiccant-dried flowers are particularly fragile (although they retain their colour and shape very well) and need to be handled with extreme care so you may wish to wire them before drying.

Fine sand

This is the heaviest substance and the slowest to take effect (up to two weeks). It should only be used for tough material. The sand must be washed and dried in an oven on a tin tray at a low temperature before use. Fine sand is sold mainly at garden centres.

Silica gel

This is less coarse than fine sand and medium-heavy material dries well in it. It actually consists of crystals which can be used many times. The crystals must be finely ground (using either a rolling pin or a pestle and mortar) before use. When dry, silica gel is blue in colour, turning pink when it has absorbed moisture. When the plant

18

material is ready (this should take between three and four days) remove it from the container and spread the crystals on a baking tray. Place the tray in a warm oven – when the crystals have turned blue again they can be cooled and stored in an airtight container for re-use.

Borax

Borax is finer still and is suitable for very delicate flowers. However, it tends to cling to the plant material and a better result can be achieved by mixing fine sand with the borax. Before mixing the two, the sand should be washed separately, thoroughly dried in an oven and then sieved together with the borax. Plant material can take up to two weeks to dry in borax.

Method

1. Put a layer of desiccant about 2.5cm (1in) deep in a suitable container (such as a plastic ice cream box) with a lid.
2. Place the material on top of the desiccant and carefully sieve and sprinkle more of it between the petals.
3. Add more desiccant to cover all the material in the container fully.
4. Put the lid on tightly and leave in a warm dry place for a few days. When fully dried, the material should feel papery. If it does not, put it back in the desiccant. When the material is ready, gently shake off all the desiccant.
5. Never store anything which has been dried in a desiccant in damp conditions of any sort.
6. After use, the desiccant must be put through a sieve, washed and thoroughly dried. Put it back in an airtight container, which is then immediately ready for use.

Glycerine

Material for glycerining should be gathered near the end of its life cycle, but not when the sap is leaving the plant. If picked too early, the material dies before it has taken up the glycerine mixture while if it has changed colour and matured too much, it has no means of taking in any moisture.

The process works by replacing the sap in the plant with glycerine. You should quickly notice the leaves and stems changing colour – when this colour change has spread over the whole piece of foliage, it is ready to be removed from the mixture. The smaller the amount of material in the glycerine, the quicker the result. This varies from a few days to a few weeks, depending on the thickness of the leaves. Some small leaves can be submerged in a large bowl. Never put grey furry leaves (such as lamb's tongue (*Stachys lanata*)) in the mixture.

Ends of stems form air locks as soon as they are picked, so they must be treated straight away. Cut the stems immediately before immersing in the glycerine mixture. If the stems are at all limp, immerse in boiling water and leave to soak overnight. When they have revived, put them in the glycerine mixture. Never immerse the leaves in boiling water.

Method

1. Make up a mixture of one-third glycerine to two-thirds boiling water and stir well.
2. Prepare the plant material as instructed on page 16 and stand the stems in a container filled to a depth of approximately 8cm (3 1/8in) with the glycerine mixture (keep this topped up to prevent the plant material from drying out). If working with large stems, first stand them in a small container of mixture and place this in turn in a bucket with enough room for the branches. Wipe over the thick leaves with the mixture to prevent too much evaporation.
3. The mixture may be reboiled, added to and used repeatedly. As soon as I have finished glycerining one lot of material, I place the flowers and foliage in a sink, sieve the used mixture into a saucepan, boil to remove any bacteria which may have formed and pour it into a clear jar for re-use. It will form a mould on the top if left too long.
4. If you want to create a bleached effect, stand the glycerined material in a bright sunny place for a few days.
5. Store glycerined material at room temperature, wrapped in tissue paper in a box, preferably with air circulating. I must admit, however, that I have stored some in a tin box in my garage for many years and it has lasted very well.

Left: Glycerined lady's mantle

Material suitable for glycerining

Alchemilla mollis (lady's mantle)

This is easy to grow and spreads well. If cut back after its first flowering it blossoms again later in the season. Cut when the star-shaped miniature flowers are fully out and slit the stem ends before placing in the glycerine mixture. The plant takes up the glycerine quickly and is ready when the florets and some of the leaves have turned brown. Stems soften so need wiring.

Buxus sempervirens (box)

This extremely useful, medium-size, slow-growing shrub glycerines beautifully but slowly. It can take several weeks before the leaves change colour to a creamy brown but it is possible to quicken the process if you first take the side stems off the main stem and immerse them separately. Remove any damaged leaves and slit the woody stems to allow them to take up the glycerine mixture.

Camellia (camellia)

Put only the leaves in the mixture. They absorb the glycerine well, turning medium to dark brown. Leaves require wiring.

Choisya ternata (Mexican orange)

The leaves glycerine beautifully, especially the smaller ones at the tops of the branches; these make good florets. Prepare small branches by cutting the stems, crushing the ends and placing them upright in the mixture. These are easy to glycerine (although slow), turning a dark-cream colour. Leave these in the mixture until moisture shows on the leaves, otherwise they become brittle when taken out. The bush should not be placed in a draughty position.

Below: Statice bouquet

Eucalyptus (eucalyptus)

Has both long and round greenish-grey foliage. Young trees are often struck down by frost. The round leaf variety is the most useful and glycerines well, not taking too long and changing to a nice brown colour. Split the stems and stand in the mixture.

Fagus sylvatica (common beech)

The glycerined branches of this deciduous tree are useful for medium and large arrangements. July is the best time to gather and glycerine beech. Branches turn fairly dark brown. They become dry and brittle if removed from the mixture too soon so should be left to stand in it until moisture appears on the leaves. Copper beech is not suitable for glycerining.

Garrya elliptica (garrya/silk tassel bush)

This evergreen shrub has long pendulous male and female catkins on separate bushes. The male ones are up to 15cm (6in) long and are suede-grey in colour. The bush dislikes being moved. The catkins glycerine well; the best time for this is when they are nearly fully grown but not yet pollinated. The leaves glycerine satisfactorily too, either on the branch or separately.

Laurus (laurel)

When glycerined, the leaves of this evergreen shrub turn a shiny brown and are most useful for swags and medium to large arrangements. The leaves do vary in size although they are mostly on the large side. The best way to glycerine laurel is to cut all but three or four leaves from a stem. Stand the stem in the glycerine mixture and immerse the individual leaves separately. These will change colour more quickly than those on

Above: Strawflower posy laid on fabric-covered board

the stems as less mixture is needed to circulate through them. The leaves will need wiring.

Mahonia aquifolium (mahonia)
The glossy dark-green leaves and stems of this evergreen shrub bring life and a sense of movement to an arrangement. Slit the stems and stand in the mixture.

Mahonia x 'Charity' (mahonia)
An evergreen shrub with leaves similar to those of *M. aquifolium* except that they are prickly, stiffer and have longer stems. Not quite so useful.

Moluccella laevis (bells of Ireland)
This half-hardy annual plant is one of the most stunning of all. The bell-shaped pods on its large stems look like flowers, but the little, insignificant flowers actually grow inside them. Remove the actual flowers after picking otherwise they will stain the green of the pods. Either hang the stems to dry or put them in the glycerine mixture. If glycerined, they will turn cream and the stems will soften, needing wiring. When dried, the pods will stay green but they may drop off and will then need to be glued back on.

Skimmia japonica (skimmia)
Some varieties of *S. japonica* are unisexual so it is necessary to grow at least one male plant for pollination – 'Foremanii', female; 'Fragans', male; Rogersii, female. It is an evergreen shrub with lovely berries. It grows well in semi-shade and the leaves glycerine to a cream colour. Slit the stem before standing it in the mixture until beads of moisture appear on the leaves.

Solidago (golden rod)
This can be glycerined. I have found in my experiments that if each spike is picked in bud and put in the glycerine mixture, it turns a nice, medium brown. Does not take long to change colour and is very useful in arrangements.

Viburnum rhytidophyllum (viburnum)
Evergreen shrub with smallish to large long leaves which are deeply veined with dark green. Leaves have grey felt-like undersides. Immerse only the leaves in the glycerine mixture; they turn dark brown quite quickly. They need wiring but are quite tender so use only thin wire. The rough-looking texture of the leaves is useful in swags and with shiny fruits.

Maintenance of dried and artificial arrangements
Most dried or artificial arrangements last a long time but they should not be kept on display indefinitely or they may become dull and dusty. The secret of keeping them in prime condition is to put them away every so often. In my own experience, it is necessary to blow the dust off them after six to eight weeks and to apply a damp cloth to the material and container if necessary after which the arrangement should be put away for a short while.

artificial fruits, flowers & foliage

Above and facing page:
Artificial fruit sprays

Below: A selection of
artificial fruits

A wide range of artificial plant material is
now readily available and, used in the right way,
it can look extremely effective and indeed realistic. It is possible to change or improve the
appearance of silk flowers and foliage with a few
simple techniques. Removing some of the outer
petals for example can transform a fully open
bloom into a bud, while skilful wiring can give a
leaf or stem a sense of movement.

Gold plastic filigree leaves are available and
these work particularly well in Christmas

arrangements. Artificial and dried fruits complement each other beautifully. The colours, shapes
and textures of artificial fruits are particularly
attractive. The leaves may be left on the stems
or taken off and wired separately. A selection of

artificial fruits laid out ready for arranging is shown below. The peach, plum, apricots, green-gages and the small bunch of pink fruits all have a wonderful bloom and could be mistaken for the real things, the pomegranates and green and blue fruits are richly coloured and the rasberries and strawberries look good enough to eat! Grapes are among the most useful fruits for arrangements but they always need to be very well wired. Many of these materials are included in the two pretty fruit sprays shown above left and right.

25

equipment & techniques

equipment

containers, stands and bases

Containers, stands and bases come in all shapes and sizes – there is such a variety that it can be difficult to make the right choice. Below is a list of some of the most useful.

Baskets
These vary enormously in size, shape and colour. Given a little know-how and a lot of patience, their potential is endless. Baskets and dried materials in particular are very popular and can complement each other perfectly. Anyone arranging dried, preserved or artificial flowers will usually want to include at least one in their repertoire.

Below: Classic and antique stands and containers such as these are very useful for flower arrangements

Boxes
A wooden box, with the lid either fully or half open to show a toning lining and containing wild flowers or fruit can be attractive. Glycerined foliage is very well suited to a box arrangement.

Brass and copper
Brass and copper or steel preserving pans, coal buckets and jugs filled with flowers can look particularly good in fireplaces, either in a traditional or a contemporary building. I feel it is easier to fit antiques into a modern house than vice versa. Dried material suits subtle-coloured containers better than bright. Old copper and brass containers look mellow whereas new ones can be far too shiny for dried materials.

Jars and vases
There is a vast array to choose from. Old or new brown jars are useful for dried arrangements. Terracotta ware is readily available and can look quite beautiful if the browns of the containers are carried through the arrangement.

Pedestals
Wooden, pottery or iron pedestals need plenty of room and are used mainly for weddings and other church occasions. Pedestal arrangements should be well balanced and must look right from all angles, including the back.

Using bases and stands
You may sometimes find these necessary for balance – if a finished arrangement seems to be

too large for its container, a base can help to bring the two into proportion. The protection of the surface on which the arrangement is going to stand is also a priority, although with dried and silk material a base may not be necessary unless the underside of the container is at all rough. The use of bases and stands in relation to the size, texture and colour scheme of the materials within the arrangement itself must be considered carefully because not all are appropriate for the task in hand. If you are not completely satisfied that the base or stand you have chosen for a particular arrangement is perfectly complementary, it is best to leave it out.

Above: A selection of modern containers which can all be used very effectively with dried, silk and paper flowers and foliage

Right: Just some of the many different types of baskets and rings available

Using a circular or oval piece of chipboard covered with fabric allows you to place extra plant material or accessories around the base of a container while ensuring that these still appear to form an integral part of the arrangement (see arrangements on pages 38 and 75). Velvet can be used to cover bases but while it certainly adds a luxurious touch, it does mark very easily. I often cover boards with Lycra and also find Dralon, particularly the more expensive type, which comes in a range of colours and does not easily crease or mark, very useful.

Carefully positioned mirrors can bring life to delicate plant material, water arrangements and to silvery leaves and flowers. Perspex pieces and wooden sections taken from tree trunks make very effective bases. Marble slabs and pedestals are ideal for silk flowers and waxed fruit, while straw or linen mats are suitable for dried fruit or glycerined material. Trays – silver plated, brass, copper and wooden – can be used very successfully, particularly if you want to include material such as bunches of grapes around the base of the container. Cork mats are useful for small Christmas arrangements with candles and holly.

Preparing containers for use
Floral or Oasis foam (the grey/brown variety rather than the green is suitable for dried and artificial material) is available in bricks, cylinders, rings and pads and is easily cut to fit most containers. It can be wedged firmly in the neck of a vase or jar, or held in place with Oasis fix, Oasis frogs, Oasis tape, wire or wire netting. The foam should always be concealed as much as possible by the plant material. To create an arrangement with space between the leaves and flowers, use moss to cover areas of exposed foam. Moss is also useful for covering wire and foam rings. It helps to establish a firm

base for the insertion of stems.

The photograph on pages 32 and 33 shows a selection of containers and mechanics. I wanted the arrangement in the shallow basket on the left to look free and uncluttered so used only one block of floral foam. To secure it, I stem taped a length of wire, folded it in half,

inserted each end through the basket from underneath on either side of the brick, brought the wire up over the brick and twisted the ends together at the top. Before tightening the wire I applied a little glue underneath the foam to fix it even more firmly in place. To finish off, I trimmed the ends of the wire and made sure

they would not catch anything.

Always choose a container in proportion to the material you are going to use. For a large arrangement, put a large block of floral foam across the centre and secure it by adding more pieces on either side as shown in the basket on the right. Do not fill the spaces completely or

Below: Some of the most useful types of base. On the left of the photograph you can see how to cover a circular base with fabric (in this case dark-green Lycra)

you will have less scope for placing the stems at different angles and levels. You can then cover the container with chicken wire, fixing it in place by weaving reel wire around the edges and tightening it as shown on the white container between the two baskets in the photograph. This stabilizes the plant material.

A foam ring should be given a fabric backing if the arrangement is to be hung on a wall. The ring on the right of the photograph was covered with a piece of green Lycra which was glued in place. A small plastic saucer with a cylindrical piece of foam secured in the centre is particularly useful for a table arrangement.

Left: Containers and mechanics

techniques

wiring

Some natural plants droop after drying no matter what method is used and so need wiring for stability in an arrangement. Artificial flowers and foliage, too, can sometimes benefit from careful wiring. Silk rose leaves for example can often seem unnaturally flat and symmetrical. You can take individual leaves or groups of leaves off the stem and wire them as shown on pages 35 and 37 to create a sense of movement. Wire provides artificial stems for cones and seedheads and added strength where the existing stems are too limp, weak or short to use effectively. Wire is also invaluable for giving shape to ribbon bows and in the construction of swags and garlands. Always try to conceal the wire as much as possible and do not choose a thicker wire than you need to provide the necessary support. With the exception of the very finest wire, gutta-percha or stem tape (available in various colours) should be twisted around the wire stem for a neat finish.

Types of wire

There are several types of wire available and each one is suited to a particular purpose.

Stub wire: This can be inserted into hollow stems or twisted round weak stems for support. It is most suitable for large flowers and seedheads and is available in a range of gauges from extra-fine to thick.

Silver rose wire: This is very fine and most useful for wiring delicate, fragile flowers and stems.

Silver reel wire: Finer still, this is used for wiring fine stems together for delicate sprays.

Wiring cones and acorns

In the top right of the photograph on page 37 I have shown a range of wired cones – these are just five types out of around two thousand! A cone's scales need to be open before wiring, so they must be wired when dry; the scales remain

closed on a wet cone. Put wire around the base between the scales, twisting the ends of the wire together to form a stem. Alnus cones grow awkwardly and are easier to use if wired together in groups of two or three. For large cones, use two pieces of wire, one on each side, and join these in the centre.

Unless acorns are taken from their cups and glued back in place they have a tendency to fall out. For those with no stalks, make false stems by holding a piece of wire over a hot flame and pushing it through the cup.

Wiring grapes

Strong wire is needed for a large bunch of artificial grapes. Wire from the centre of the main stem and use at least two thick wires.

Wiring silk, paper and natural flowers

Silk hydrangeas are amazingly realistic. You can cut small groups or even individual flowers and wire and stem tape them either fully open or in bud-like form. It is sometimes difficult to find suitable blue flowers to use in arrangements so silk hydrangeas are particularly useful for their pale, delicate colour. Paper flowers such as the pink and the white rose shown in the photograph on page 36 tend not to need wiring.

1. Wired chiffon-patterned ribbon bow
2. Wired cones (alnus and pine)
3. Wired silk roses
4. Silk carnations (one with outer petals removed for a bud-like form)
5. Varnished poppy seedhead
6. Wired silk rose leaves
7. Silk rose leaves before wiring

Right: A selection of natural and artificial materials wired and stem taped, wired or ready for wiring

I usually wire strawflowers (*Helichrysum*) through the base of the flowers before drying, though some people prefer to hook the wire through the centres. After wiring, they should be stem taped. Dried achillea (*Achillea*) is extremely useful for natural-looking arrangements and, again, small pieces can be wired and stem taped quite easily.

Wiring leaves

Silk rose leaves can be made to look more natural if they are wired tightly at the base so that they are slightly furled or if they are grouped in twos and threes. Glycerined ivy (*Hedera*) leaves benefit from careful wiring – they can be folded slightly to give the impression of movement and then stem taped. Another method of wiring leaves is to take a piece of wire and twist it once or twice around the stem. Then make a small stitch across the main central vein at the back. Bring the wire down the stem again and twist the two ends together.

Wiring buds

Senecio (*S. greyi*) and magnolia (*Magnolia*) buds are easily dried and have a soft fur-like texture which is very useful for certain types of arrangement. To strengthen these, wire should be wound around the existing stems.

Wire twirls

Wire twirls, such as the two shown on the right, can often lend textural interest and a sense of movement to an arrangement. They are easily made by stem taping lengths of stub wire and curling these around a pencil.

colour spraying

Almost any dried or glycerined material can be sprayed gold, silver or bronze if it is in good condition. I tend to use Oasis Spray (available from florists and garden centres) for this. Larger items, such as pine cones, usually acquire a brighter appearance if they are brushed over with white distemper before gilding. Foliage, seedheads and cereals (such as oats and wheat) look very attractive when gilded.

Above left: Vase, silk flowers and spray colour

Above right: The finished arrangement. The vase was first sprayed moss-green. Touches of purple and gold were then added to pick up on the colour scheme of the flowers

In addition, it is possible to spray certain containers in order to highlight or emphasise colours within the arrangement itself. The white vase used for the arrangement shown above would have looked too stark against the rich, vibrant colours of the silk flowers and leaves. I decided that colouring it first with moss-green Oasis spray and then with a light spray of purple, finishing with a touch of gold would transform the vase completely. When finished, the vase carried the colour scheme from top to bottom while ensuring that the flowers themselves were not overpowered.

1. Glycerined box
2. Dried stinking iris
3. Dried corn
4. Dried wheat
5. Dried *Silaum silaus* seedheads
6. Silk holly leaf
7. Plastic filigree leaves
8. Glycerined laurel leaf
9. Cedar cone
10. Poppy seedhead
11. Dried stinking iris
12. Dried stinking iris
13. Alnus cone
14. Dried quince
15. Plastic holly leaf
16. Dried alnus catkins
17. Acorn

waxing crepe paper flowers

Any crepe paper flower is suitable for waxing. Do take care when heating wax, especially if there are children or animals around; the hot drips may burn the skin.

Equipment
Pale-coloured and white candles
Double boiler or heavy saucepan
Newspaper
Oasis
Paper flowers

Method
1. For an economical waxing liquid, melt down used or broken coloured and white candles. Stick to the lighter colours and use only white candles for white flowers. Place the candles in the top of a double boiler or in a heavy saucepan over a gentle heat.
2. When the candles have melted, remove their wicks with a fork. The wax should never be hot enough to smoke or to burn your fingers badly. Keep it in liquid form, turning the heat down or up as required.
3. Have some Oasis foam ready so the wired waxed flower can be placed in it to solidify without touching anything. Spread newspaper underneath to catch any drips.
4. Make sure the flower is complete in every detail and then dip it in wax making sure that all the petals are coated. Take the flower out (remember: dip, don't soak) and shake it gently to remove any surplus.

5. Repeat this process as soon as the wax on the flower is set.
6. Keep repeating until you have achieved the result you want.

Waxed oriental poppy

Follow these instructions for a realistic poppy.

Equipment
Packets of folded red and black crepe paper or other colours of your choice.
Water
Newspaper
Scissors and glue
Tracing paper
Thin reel wire (see page 34)
Waxing equipment

Method
1. Remove a sheet of crepe paper (use the old type rather than the thick crinkly type) from the packet but do not unfold it. Cut strips of this paper across the grain. You can cut two, three or four strips from the paper depending on the size of the petals required. Then cut strips of the same size in brown, black, dark green or whatever colour/s you think suitable. The flower in the photograph on page 41 was made with a mixture of red and black crepe paper.
2. Unfold the first colour and then unfold and place the other colour/s on top of the

dominant one. Now refold the strips as they were before you opened them out, wet them right through to the middle and gently squeeze the moisture and colour through. Unfold them carefully, as the dye will run, place them on newspaper and leave them, preferably in a warm place, to dry.

3. When the paper is dry, its texture is stronger. The colours will merge and become interesting. You can experiment with large and small poppies, other flowers and a whole range of ideas, creating most unusual colours.

4. Sketch a petal pattern like the one shown in the photograph opposite, cut it out and stick it on to a piece of thin cardboard. You can use this as a template over and over again. Cut four petals for each poppy (with the grain running from top to bottom) from the dried refolded paper. You can cut more than one at a time.

5. Flute each petal three or four times by easing and pulling the top edge between your finger and thumb, turning it over to form a lightly frilled edge. Then make a cut at the bottom centre of the petal. Glue along one side of the cut, pull the other edge over and press firmly together in order to make the petal slightly cup shaped.

6. For the centre of the poppy, crush and roll some spare crepe paper into a small ball or use a piece of cotton wool. Stretch a 7cm (2 3/4in) square of black crepe paper over the ball, pinching it tightly underneath. Flatten the top slightly by pressing on it and wire the base with reel wire.

7. Cut through the folded layers of some black crepe paper to make a strip 4.5cm (1 3/4in) wide. Stretch it out and make 2.5cm (1in) cuts all the way along one edge to form a fringe. Roll the cut ends between thumb and forefinger to separate the strands of the fringe. Wind this strip round the ball until it is covered, then cut off any surplus paper and wire one end with thin reel wire.

8. Put a little glue on the lower part of each of the four petals and place them evenly around the centre, overlapping them slightly. Then wire the base of the flower again with fine reel wire. Take a cocktail stick or a long piece of stub wire and stem tape the poppy on to this, making sure everything is held firmly in place by the wire at the base of the poppy.

9. Follow the instructions on page 40 for waxing.

Right: Making an oriental poppy
1. Petal template
2. Crepe paper petals
3. Poppy centre
4. Wired poppy centre
5. Two finished poppies wired and stem taped

making cone and topiary trees

Cone and topiary trees are very pretty and can be made using a wide range of dried or artificial material, or a combination of the two. They range from being tall and ornate to small and simple and can be put in decorative or plain pots. They should last for many years but although they are neither difficult nor expensive to make, it can take some time to prepare and wire all the material you will need. They can look wonderful on an antique side table or a mantlepiece – experiment to find out which situation suits it best.

Trees become almost twice their original size when completed, so the floral foam should be smaller than the size of the container, otherwise the finished arrangement will appear top heavy. Also, when positioning the central stick, allow extra space for material to be placed between the stick and the container. Terracotta plant pots are ideal for artificial trees, but any sort of container, provided it is a sensible size and suits the arrangement you have in mind, can be used. Plant pots can be used as they are or painted, covered in material (velvet is useful), or glue and coarse sand can be applied. Plastic pots are the easiest to cover and terracotta ones are best for taking glue and sand.

Method

1. Measure and mark the height of your container on to your chosen stick. Add the length needed between the top of the container and the Oasis and the length needed for inserting the stick roughly half-way up through the middle of the Oasis.

2. Cut the stick to the required length and carve it to a point at one end. If it is a thick, heavy stick, hammer three nails into one end, otherwise the Oasis will crumble as you insert the stick, providing little support for the stems. Leave the other end blunt. The pointed or nailed end should be inserted into the Oasis; the flat end stands at the bottom of the container.

3. If you wish, cover the stick with crepe stem tape, either green or brown according to the type of tree you wish to make and your chosen colour scheme.

4. Mix some Polyfilla or plaster of Paris in accordance with the instructions. Work quickly through the next step before the mixture hardens.

5. Place the stick in the plant pot with a few stones around it for stability (this is especially necessary if you are using a plastic pot).

6. Fill two-thirds of the pot with the setting mixture, covering the stones. Make sure the stick is perfectly upright – by lining it up with a kitchen cupboard door, for example – and leave it to set, preferably over night.

7. Glue the stick from the pointed end to half the depth of the Oasis and insert it in the Oasis, making sure it is dead centre. Leave to dry, again overnight.

8. Cover the top of the container with moss or decorative pebbles if you wish.

9. Prepare and wire your flowers, foliage, seedheads and any ribbon bows or roses and insert them into the Oasis.

ribbons and bows

Ribbons and bows are perfect for arrangements for special occasions such as birthdays and anniversaries. Bows need to be crisp and their ends must curl nicely, otherwise they will detract from rather than enhance an arrangement. The first step to achieving an attractive result is to use suitable ribbon.

Toning ribbon with an intricate arrangement takes practice. Sometimes using a small amount of colour in the arrangement and highlighting it with the ribbon works well. Neutral colours are usually safer than bright ones as the latter can overwhelm any delicate material. The width of the ribbon is important as all the components of the arrangement must be in proportion.

If a bow is used for a gift arrangement, it may dominate quite happily. However, it will be less conspicuous if it is positioned first. This turns the ribbon into a component of the whole design, so it looks as if it belongs.

Ribbons

There is an enormous variety of ribbon available. I find the following very useful.

Grosgrain ribbon: This is crisp, stable and available in solid colours, patterns and stripes. It is useful for bows and roses.

Hessian ribbon: Wide, threaded hessian ribbon comes in a range of pleasant colours which are not over-bright.

Metallic ribbon: Used mainly at Christmas, available colours include gold, blue, red, silver and green.

Paper ribbon: This is especially suitable for swags and wreaths. It makes solid bows and is useful for heavy material.

Rolled paper ribbon: This can be unwound to whatever width is required, or used as it comes. Its texture and colours are compatible with dried material. Some patterns are very pretty.

Satin ribbon: With a seam on each side to prevent fraying, this is well worth buying. It can be shiny on one side only or on both and is good for making bows and roses.

Velvet ribbon: This type of ribbon is available in superb colours. It has a lovely texture, but is limp when tied in a bow unless it is lined with satin.

Wired-edge ribbon: This is available in delightful patterns and also in plain. It is very useful for bows and roses.

100% polyester ribbon: A very fine ribbon, available in beautiful colours and good patterns. It makes lovely bows but needs to be used with delicate material.

Bows

Ribbon bows are incredibly useful and versatile. They hold their shape well, can be placed in Oasis and wired on to swags or into any part of an arrangement. Any width of ribbon may be used.

Method

1. If you have never made a bow before, choose a wired-edge ribbon 2.5cm (1in) wide with one plain side. This will help you keep the ribbon folding in the right direction.

Top: Making a bow
Centre: A completed, wired and stem taped ribbon bow; two sets of wired and stem taped ribbon roses; three ways of cutting ribbon ends
Bottom: Making a ribbon rose

47

2. Cut a 76cm (30in) length. Also cut a 25.5cm (10in) length of medium gauge reel wire and keep handy. Note: left handers should substitute right for left and vice versa.

3. Hold one end of the length of ribbon in your left hand, between thumb and index finger. Hold the other end away from you in your right hand, plain side up. Using your right hand make a loop (judging the size of the loop gets easier with practice), taking the end of the ribbon over to the left. Leave enough ribbon at the bottom (short end) of the loop for one end of the bow.

4. Holding the first loop in place between your right thumb and index finger, bring the end of the ribbon in your left hand up over your right thumb to make a second loop of equal size to the first, patterned side up.

5. Fold the long piece under to form the third loop (which will be diagonally opposite the second), taking the end of the ribbon underneath the centre.

6. Take the end of the ribbon back over the centre to form the fourth loop (between the first and second). Adjust the loops slightly to ensure that the ends of the bow are of equal length or cut one end to match the other.

7. Anchor the loops firmly in your right hand and then concertina the centre of the bow.

8. Take up the wire in your right hand and wire round the centre once, placing the wire first under and round the first two loops, then under and round the third and fourth.

9. Secure tightly and twist the wire together to the end of its length, forming a stem.

10. Tidy up the bow and bring the loops forward to hide the wire. It is not necessary to bind the stem, but you can if you wish.

Left: A pretty, delicate posy made from four types of ribbon

Ribbon rose

There are several ways to make a ribbon rose. The ones shown on page 47 are pretty and easy to make. The width of the ribbon can be varied from 2.5cm (1in) to 10-12.5cm (4-5in).

Method

1. Cut a 30.5 (12in) length of 2.5cm (1in) wide fine-wired ribbon. Also cut a 20cm (8in) length of medium-gauge reel wire.

2. Hold the ribbon vertically and turn the top end over to the left to form a small triangle.

3. With both hands, tightly roll the triangle down towards the lower end of the piece of ribbon four to six times to form a centre for the rose. Hold the rose centre firmly in your left hand and turn it upright so that the length of ribbon is now horizontal.

4. With your right hand, fold the ribbon back to form a triangle – the length of ribbon is now pointing downwards. Working in a clockwise direction, lift and take the triangle round to the left of the rose centre. You have formed the first petal and should now be holding the end of the ribbon out to the right.

5. Make four or five petals in the same way, pushing the centre of the rose down level with the petals as you work.

6. When you have made enough petals (don't try to make more than you can easily handle or your rose will disintegrate!), bring the last piece of ribbon forward and hold it in front.

7. Still holding the rose with the left hand, wire directly under it taking in a little ribbon.

8. Cut the end of the ribbon at a slant and twist the rest of the wire together over the ribbon, forming a stem.

9. Bind the stem with stem tape.

arrangements

the natural look

sugar caddy

Facing page: A pretty arrangement made from dried grasses, poppy seedheads and leaves

For this arrangement, grasses and leaves of a similar colour to the sugar caddy were chosen. I thought the arrangement should look the same from every angle and started by putting the tall and short grasses in to form the basic shape.

A contrast with the long, feathery grasses was provided by the poppy (*Papaver*) seedheads, Jerusalem sage (*Phlomis fruticosa*), love-lies-bleeding (*Amaranthus)* and, over the rim, a few dried lime (*Tilia* x *europaea*) leaves. Some of the grasses and dock (*Rumex*) seedheads were tinged with mauve, so to emphasise this colour some mauve wild thistle-type dried flowers were added. To keep the arrangement in proportion I placed the sugar caddy on a wooden base.

brown caddy

Even slight variations in colour, shape and size of material can alter the appearance of an arrangement. Grasses, poppy (*Papaver*) seed-heads and leaves were used in both the sugar caddy (page 52) and this brown caddy, but the poppy seedheads were shades of grey and brown in the latter rather than the green used in the former, creating a bolder look.

This tall, narrow jar called for a higher arrangement than that used for the sugar caddy, and the dark-brown base just helped to bring everything together.

Facing page: A natural-looking arrangement of dried materials

baskets

continental arrangement

The shape of this basket made it suitable for a Continental arrangement. The material needed to be portrayed as though it was growing and I wanted to create the impression that air could circulate throughout. As in a typical Continental-style arrangement, each type of material was grouped and some of the leaves were placed horizontally. I used dried green safflower (*Carthamus*) buds and artifical jonquils (*Narcissus*), two medium-sized silk pink flowers, silk gentians (*Gentiana*) and crocuses (*Crocus*), begonia (*Begonia*) leaves and variegated ivy (*Hedera*) leaves, ferns, a small contorted willow twig (*Salix matsudana* 'Tortuosa') and a piece of weathered wood.

Right: Interestingly-shaped and textured pieces of bark or wood such as the one seen here and in the Continental arrangement on the facing page are very versatile and can be used in a variety of different ways

Facing page: A striking arrangement in the Continental style

mother's day basket

Create this natural-looking arrangement with silk buttercups (*Ranunculus*) and violets (*Viola*) as follows.

1. Cut a small cylindrical piece of Oasis in half and glue it into the basket with Copydex (you may find a glue gun handy for this).

2. Glue a small amount of reindeer moss all over the Oasis.

3. Wire the leaves and flowers of both butter-cups and violets and tape the stems.

4. Place five of each of the two leaf types in the basket facing in different ways.

5. Finally, put in the pale and dark violets and the buttercups, creating a balance between the brighter and more delicate colours.

Right: This little basket filled with buttercups and violets would make the perfect gift for Mother's Day or Easter

easter basket

Without a handle, this basket was more squat than deep, so the arrangement itself could not be too high. Three pieces of Oasis were required: one whole piece put across the centre of the basket widthways, and one, slightly trimmed, on either side.

I chose traditional Easter colours for this arrangement and began by putting in the wired glycerined and silk leaves and then the mauve silk irises (*Iris*). This filled quite a gap, but it still needed something extra so I added some dried yellow and mauve achillea (*Achillea*) and some mauve statice (*Limonium sinuata*). Yellow and orange safflower (*Carthamus*) buds and mauve dried blazing star (*Liatris*) were then added. I completed the arrangement with two green, open-weave cotton ribbon bows which carried the green of the foliage down on either side of the basket.

The purple flowers decorating the front of the basket were cut from furnishing fabric, dipped in fabric stiffener (available from craft shops and flower arranging suppliers) and pressed firmly into position. They were then left to dry and spray varnished.

Right: The lilac and yellow colour scheme works beautifully in this arrangement and is carried down on to the basket itself

basket with peonies and wheat

It takes quite a lot to fill a large basket such as this one, so you need to lay out all your material in advance to check that you have enough. This is a fairly deep, rich chestnut-coloured basket without handles, equally suited to tall or short flowers, foliage, grasses and seedheads. To fill it completely with either dried or silk flowers would be both expensive and hard work, so I chose some richly-coloured silk peonies (*Paeonia*) which complemented the basket, plus imported wooden flowers, large, dried pinkish protea (*Protea*) buds, bronze onion (*Allium*) seed-heads, and dock (*Rumex*) seedheads. The heights of all these were varied.

I used the dried wheat (*Triticum*) for its blend-ing colour and texture, the curling leaves on its stems giving a lovely sense of movement. I then inserted the dock seedheads and the large wired glycerined and silk leaves into the Oasis, placing some over the front of the basket.

Right: A beautiful richly-coloured arrangement – ideal for brightening up a hall or fireplace

basket with wild roses & blackberries

Only a small, square piece of brown Oasis was needed for this medium-sized oblong basket because I wanted a fairly free, loose arrangement with small spaces showing at each end. The Oasis was glued inside the bottom of the basket and then secured with wire.

The artificial wild roses (*Rosa*) went in first, with their leaves already wired to the stems. A small group of rose leaves, chosen for their natural colour and shape, was fixed in the middle to carry the green right through the arrangement. I then included artificial blackberry (*Rubus*) sprays with their leaves and tendrils along the centre of the arrangement, taking up the wild natural look of the roses. I thought the texture and colour of the pink ribbon complemented the roses very well, so made two bows, placing one at each side of the basket, though another flower and more leaves would have sufficed.

Right: Just like the arrangement on page 59, this charming little basket of wild roses and blackberries would make a perfect gift

basket with peonies and fruit

This basket with a reinforced steel base and handle is beautifully made. Finding suitable material was a challenge though, as turquoise is a difficult colour to match. Picking up both the colours of the basket and of the steel fittings was my first thought.

It is a heavy basket, so it obviously needed filling with large flowers or fruit. The lovely cream silk peonies (*Paeonia*) went very well with the pale-coloured wicker and the small, blue artificial fruit bunches toned in with the handle. Wired artificial pomegranates and plums complemented the rest of the material, while the wired light-brown silk leaves taken from the peony stems, the glycerined beech (*Fagus sylvatica*) leaves and the fir tree pieces picked up the two browns of the basket. The muted colour scheme, the soft bloom of the fruits and the rounded shapes created a harmonious result, helping the eye to travel easily over all the material.

Right: The cream silk peonies used in this arrangement show how natural-looking and how beautiful artificial flowers can be

round lacquered wicker box

I found this box in a garden centre, along with the matching artificial nasturtiums (*Tropaeolum*) – the two were just meant for each other.

I cut two bricks of brown Oasis to fit the box tightly across the centre, and stood the lid at the back. The nasturtiums and leaves were arranged first, with some flowing over the sides. The dried oats (*Avena*), which had been left in the sun to turn a natural pale brown, picking up the colour of the raffia, were then positioned to give the arrangement extra height and to add a light, feather-like shape. The glycerined lady's mantle (*Alchemilla mollis*), which had turned a pretty brown, lightened the whole effect texturally.

Left and facing page: A simple setting is needed to offset the strong, vibrant colours in an arrangement like this. A bright, spacious conservatory is ideal

fruits

exotic fruit basket

When I saw this floral drape, I knew straight away that it would complement the basket and fruit I already had. The colour of the basket matched the blue-green of the fabric particularly well and its circular shape did not conflict with the large, bold pink flowers on the material. The small opening at the top of the basket allowed room for only a limited amount of material, so I was able to use relatively expensive artificial fruit.

The fruits, including the grapes, were wired and arranged first, the main aims being to achieve an attractive colour combination and a good balance between the round shapes and the more pointed ones. I allowed some bunches of grapes to tumble over the front of the basket and positioned several silk leaves to break up the solid clusters of fruit. Finally, I worked some bows of gold openwork ribbon into the arrangement but left the ornate handle showing. The colours were muted overall.

Facing page: The range of colours and textures used in this arrangement is simply stunning

fruit tree in red container

I puzzled over the best way to use this container. It seemed at first that it was too small and its red too dominant for a modern arrangement – a little fruit tree was the perfect solution.

I find it useful to collect cones, acorns, beechnuts etc. of different sizes and shapes and to store these away for possible future use. It is also worthwhile collecting small artificial fruits, buying them a few at a time to keep in reserve. For this arrangement, I used between twenty and forty of each type of material. When making trees such as this one, try not to use too many varieties, although a combination of rough and smooth textures works well.

After constructing the basic tree (see page 44), small pieces of foliage were wired and positioned around the base of the tree so that there would be a soft line at the bottom of the cone rather than a hard, straight edge. I left a space in each quarter to break up the fan-type look, putting pieces of wired glycerined conifer and the larger fruits in these spaces. I then worked up and around the tree, placing in the wired fir cones.

The main colour needed to be established, and that, of course, was red, the colour of the base. All the red fruits were placed in different positions around the tree, ending with a small pointed red fruit at the top. I then gradually filled the tree with foliage and the other coloured fruits.

With cone and topiary trees, there are always a number of gaps which can be difficult to fill. In this instance, small red berries were wired into bunches and put in strategic positions; bringing them forward helped create a three-dimensional look. Other spaces were filled with poppy (*Papaver*) seedheads and small, interestingly-shaped cones. Do not put in too many different types of material or the tree will look cluttered and over-fussy. I completed this tree by varnishing small washed stones and gluing them at the top of the red container. Finally, four wired red ribbon bows were placed underneath the cone at the front of each quarter.

Trees such as this should never be hurried as they need rather a lot of attention. Before deciding that an arrangement is complete, look at it from every angle – both sitting down and standing up, and particularly from the top. It often comes as a surprise to find just how many little gaps still need filling.

Facing page: A cone tree decorated with pretty, brightly-coloured berries and ribbons – perfect for Christmas

fruit in black comports

I found these black comports in a large department store and felt they would be just right for a fruit arrangement. They were fairly cheap so I bought two and decided to use both together. I secured one on top of the other with Oasis fix (see pages 30 and 32), and glued a round Oasis in the top bowl and smaller pieces cut from an Oasis block to the bottom edge of the top container to hold the fruit in position.

I used a combination of artificial and natural materials and separated the fruit into yellows and greens at the top and reds underneath, distributing textures fairly evenly. I find that putting two dull colours together, then one shiny and then one dull or rough texture and so on, removes any trace of monotony, as does the addition of bunches of smaller fruits and grapes. It is also a good idea to put a few leaves in a fruit arrangement. They separate the the larger pieces and a pointed leaf can offset a round fruit and vice versa. Use them sparingly, however, as too many leaves can spoil an effect.

This arrangement definitely needed a base for balance. I chose a chipboard base covered in black fabric and edged with brown brocade and placed a bunch of grapes on either side.

Facing page: In this arrangement it is almost impossible to tell the artificial and real fruits apart. The plain black comports provide the ideal background for such a lavish display of colour

vases

dark-blue vase

I envisaged this as a rather dramatic arrangement, the container being tall, elegant and a strong colour. To create this effect, I used pieces cut from a large branch of contorted willow (*Salix matsudana* 'Tortuosa') salvaged when it was blown down in a park near my house.

I prepared the vase by gluing a round piece of Oasis sideways into the neck. This gave the contorted willow twigs plenty of depth for stability and me less Oasis to fill. Each willow twig was cut to a point at one end for easy insertion into the Oasis. They looked right the first time I placed them, so I immediately glued them firmly in position. After the twigs had set, I carefully straightened out the leaves and petals of three silk lilies (*Lilium*) and placed them at varying heights in the centre of the foam. They were arranged so that the tallest semi-closed lily pointed straight up, the next (more open) one was tilted slightly forwards, and the lowest one was bent to the right. Finally, I cut three large silk leaves from the main stem of a variegated fatsia (*Fatsia*) plant, wired them and placed them at the neck of the vase.

Tip: If a small piece of Oasis still shows after you have completed and are satisfied with your arrangement, conceal it by gluing on a little reindeer or dried moss.

Facing page: This simple arrangement made with only contorted willow twigs, lilies and fatsia leaves makes a real impact

grey vase with cream lilies and peonies

The grey vase was more bulbous than the dark-blue one shown on page 77 and needed a wider arrangement for balance. It did not call for very delicate material although the volume required meant that it did need a larger amount of Oasis than the blue vase. I cut and glued a large block of Oasis to fit the neck of the vase completely and in order to accommodate the material I wanted to fall over the front of the vase, I left at least 2.5cm (1in) of Oasis protruding from the neck.

The dried dock (*Rumex*) seedheads and lime (*Tilia* x *europaea*) twigs were arranged first to establish an outline. Next, cream silk lilies (*Lilium*) and medium-sized peonies (*Paeonia*) and their buds were put in, some of each falling over the top edge of the vase. Finally, I carefully wired two dried hosta (*Hosta*) leaves and placed these at the front.

Facing page: This arrangement shows just how well silk flowers and dried foliage can be made to complement each other

cones

white column cone

Above: A combination of natural and artificial material in delicate shapes and colours is used in this arrangement

Columns such as the one shown here are very widely available and are particularly suitable for cone arrangements. Glue a brown Oasis cone to the top of a column and leave it for at least four hours to set. Arranging cones is a matter of individual taste. I prefer to establish the main colours first – in this instance the white of the column and the pink of the six wired satin bows which I made and positioned at intervals around the base. I put these in first so further material would cover some ribbon as I intended to show only a little pink at the base of the cone.

Next came the pink silk roses (*Rosa*), the white ribbon roses and the everlasting daisies (*Helipterum*) with yellow centres. The grapes, which were tinged with pink, were wired in tiny bunches, larger ones at the base, smaller ones higher up and around the cone. I then added the wired stems of yellow achillea (*Achillea*), which took up the colour of the centres of the white everlasting daisies. I fixed dried wired senecio (*S. greyi)* in strategic places, with one piece at the top, and then positioned the wired silk and glycerined leaves. A few lighter brown wired seedheads were added to effect the transition from the dark-brown cones and beech nuts to the cream of the dried meadowsweet *(Filipendula ulmaria)*. A round base covered with pinkish-brown Dralon was placed underneath the white column for balance and to carry the pink downwards.

frog cone

Above: White satin ribbon roses add a pretty touch to this charming cone arrangement

Even though this little frog was broken, I could not resist buying him with the intention of using him for a cone arrangement. To prepare the base for use, a brown Oasis cone was glued firmly to the top where a candlestick had once stood and left to set.

I first followed the line of the cornucopia the frog was holding with a tall curved stalk of grass. Dried and artificial materials were selected to match the shades of grey, green, white, lemon and cerise on the frog and were gradually worked into the arrangement. The leaves at the base were cut from bunches of artificial grapes, wired separately and inserted at different angles.

I separated a large bunch of small, green artificial grapes into clusters of various sizes and wired and graded them up the cone, with the largest at the base and the smallest at the top. Next I added some sea holly (*Eryngium*) and wild meadowsweet (*Filipendula ulmaria*); the rough textures provided a good contrast with the shiny grapes. The strawflowers (*Helichrysum*) carried the yellow, white and cerise throughout the arrangement. Finally, I positioned some cream ribbon roses and tiny artificial apples around the cone.

small gold figure cone

This was a very economical arrangement, its base being a small, green plastic figure. I glued an Oasis cone to the platform at the top of the figure which was then sprayed gold.

Small pine cones and acorns, glued to their cups and gilded, formed the bulk of the material. Narrow gold ribbon bows were wired and put around the cone and small bunches of gold berries were fixed to hang down from the sides. The gold openwork leaves were wired in last to create more textural variation.

Tip: Do not spray gold ribbon or openwork leaves because they lose all their interest if there is no variation in the colour of the gold used in the arrangement.

Below: For this arrangement, everything except the openwork leaves and ribbon bows, which were added last, was sprayed gold

candles & candlesticks

mechanics & arrangements

Before using candles, it is important to assess their type, size and colour in relation to both the holder and the material you wish to use. I have seen many arrangements where the candles were not tall enough; I actually prefer them to be too tall rather than too short!

Cylindrical Oasis is useful for arrangements with candlesticks and candles. To prepare it, work through the steps below.

1. Cut across a cylindrical Oasis to the depth you need, place the candle dead centre, mark round the base of the candle and then cut the marked piece out.

2. Using a knife, cut the Oasis at a slant around its top edge.

3. Put the candle through the hole. This then, of course, fits into the candlestick making everything firm. You can glue the Oasis to the candlestick if you prefer.

The photograph opposite shows a selection of candlestick arrangements – both complete and incomplete – and the mechanics needed for each one.

Tape cocktail sticks around the base of a large candle so that you do not have to cut a large hole in the Oasis. On smaller candles, cut a point at the base and insert this into the Oasis. Fit brass or black candle cups on candlesticks and conceal them with plant material.

I felt that the black openwork wrought iron candlestick (far left) called for an arrangement which would twist elegantly down from top to bottom. The medium-sized grapes with their attractive velvety bloom were perfect for the job, and I used a black chiffon bow for a delicate, semi-transparent look. A satin bow would have been too heavy and sombre, particularly with the solid black candle.

For the pewter candlestick (second from left) I chose a tall, slender bright-red candle, some variegated holly, a red ribbon rose, an openwork ribbon bow and a solid ribbon bow. The posy lying near the base of the candlestick has been wired ready for inserting in the Oasis next to the first bunch of material.

I chose a dark-green candle for the pottery candlestick in the centre of the photograph, and put two patterned wired bows at either side of it. Then I arranged dried orange strawflowers (*Helichrysum*), silk yellow buttercups (*Ranunculus*) and small leaves, and dried cones and poppy (*Papaver*) seedheads at the base of the candle, inserting them into the Oasis secured there.

At first sight, it might seem that the ornate brass candlestick (second from right) would suit a fancy or twisted candle. However, I found the tall, plain gold one far more complementary as it did not overwhelm the candlestick.

A thin candle would have looked completely lost in the green-gold candlestick on the right of the photograph. I tried using a large white candle

but, apart from its size, it did not seem right. So, using watercolours, I painted it first green, then blue in a rough-textured way and, finally, lightly sprayed it with gold. I was fortunate enough to have a ribbon of the right width which was also a perfect colour match and, having made it into a bow, I placed it at the base of the candle. The bunch of small gold grapes draped down the front of the candlestick reduced the rather straight, thick appearance of the candle.

Above: When you have chosen the most suitable candle for the candlestick you wish to use, decide what mechanics (from the selection shown here) you need for the type of arrangement you have in mind

special occasion pair

I purchased this pair of candles at the same time and in the same place as the large peach and grey candle on page 89. I decided to make a different type of arrangement to go with these candles because they were much narrower, fitting comfortably into a pair of Regency candlesticks. I chose pink and brown as the colour scheme.

First of all, I covered an oval chipboard base in pink Dralon and then took some pink artificial gladioli (*Gladiolus*) flowers off their main stems and wired them individually. Two rather fancy silk anemones (*Anemone*) were put in for extra interest, as were the berries and the poppy (*Papaver*) seedheads. Leaves of varying shapes, sizes and colours (from cream to brown and green) were placed in appropriate positions within the arrangement.

I felt that the colour scheme would benefit if the gilt of the candlesticks could be picked up with a little gold somewhere in the arrangement. However, gold flowers and foliage did not actually look right, so instead I pinned a decorative gold edging all the way around the base. Pinning rather than gluing allows you to remove the edging easily for a different type of arrangement.

Above: In the right surroundings, arrangements made to go with candlesticks can provide a touch of elegance

Right: This arrangement picks up on the pale pink of the candles while the pretty gold edging around the base complements the gilt candlesticks beautifully

mauve candles

Such a large arrangement is better suited to three or more thin candles than one large one. The base in this instance was a piece of kidney-shaped chipboard covered in mauve Dralon. Before gluing a piece of Oasis in place, I stapled through the Dralon fabric at the centre of the board to prevent it from lifting.

I cut the candles to three different heights with a point at the base of each one, placing the tallest at the back and leaving a small space between them. (When positioning candles, make sure they stand perfectly upright.) I made two chiffon-patterned ribbon bows and placed one at the front and one at the back of the trio of candles and then arranged the largest stiff mauve silk flowers. Next I added paler silk flowers and a few smaller ones, together with some buds. The well-wired mauve grapes were put in at either side and the silk leaves then completed the effect.

Left: Here, the pink and lilac colour scheme tones perfectly with the tall, slim, mauve candles

white candle

I put a small arrangement between the candle and the candlestick to break the long vertical column of white. Decorated with green and gold material, this elegant candlestick would make a perfect centrepiece for a Christmas dinner table.

First I placed the wired light- and dark-green ribbon bows on each side of the candle. The dark-green ribbon was seamed along both edges to prevent fraying and the light-green ribbon was edged with wire, enabling the bows to retain their shape. I then wired in the small gilded pine cones and poppy (*Papaver*) seedheads, the gold artificial acorns and leaves, together with a few green berries, and some bunches of small white dried bellflowers (*Campanula lactiflora* 'Loddon Anna'). A small spray of similar material added interest at the base.

Right: For a sophisticated table centrepiece on a special occasion, try decorating a candlestick with small bunches of flowers, leaves and cones, adding ribbons to bring everything together

wreaths

peach wreath

When using an Oasis wreath (see page 33), glue either felt or Lycra on to its back before commencing your arrangement. This will protect the wall or piece of furniture on which it will eventually hang or stand. Always make sure, before you begin, that you have enough plant material to complete the arrangement because wreath rings must be well covered and fairly symmetrical or they will look confused.

Left: A beautiful wreath made with a variety of dried and artificial material. The four peach chiffon bows soften the outline slightly

candle and wreath

I bought this beautiful hand-made candle at an arts and crafts fair and, with some persuasion, I managed to acquire the stand at the same time. The fact that the stand was so suitable helped me to create just the right arrangement for the candle. I used an Oasis ring backed with felt (see page 33), and checked I had enough plant material to cover it completely.

The peach and grey colours of the candle needed to be picked up in the wreath. First, six large silk peach roses (*Rosa*) were placed around the wreath ring at equal distances, together with bunches of smaller silk flowers of a similar colour, establishing a fairly loose pattern. The four bows of peach chiffon ribbon were fixed around the perimeter and glycerined leaves and small pieces of glycerined conifer were put in the spaces around the outside edge between the bows; these were taken through the wreath and also used to fill the inner edge. Next the poppy (*Papaver*) seedheads, pine cones and small bunches of black grapes were wired in. Lastly, I found the grey, which picked up the colour of the lower section of the candle, in wired dried senecio (*S. greyi*) buds plus leaves of lamb's tongue (*Stachys lanata*). I put the wreath over the candle and stand, and raised the whole arrangement to the right height by placing it on a peach-covered chipboard base of the same diameter as the wreath.

Above: Although it is customary to pin wreaths on doors, they can also look very effective when placed on a flat surface over a candlestick

gold and peach wreath

Facing page: This gold and peach wreath makes a delightful alternative to the traditional Christmas holly wreath

All the material on this natural twig wreath was wired to the frame. To begin with, gold ribbon bows were placed at the top and on either side. Gold Christmas roses (*Helleborus*) were placed at the top and sides of the wreath ring and two gold roses (*Rosa*) were positioned at the top right. Gold leaves were then fixed almost all the way around the wreath while gilded cones and poppy (*Papaver*) seedheads provided rough textures, reducing much of the brightness of the gold. Finally, two pretty bows of gold ribbon were placed at the base of the ring and three pinkish-red pomegranates, two peaches and four pink hessian ribbon roses were wired in around the ring for extra colour.

Tip: While working on a wreath, hang it on a wall from time to time to check that it is well balanced and that none of the material is loose.

christmas arrangements

gold swag

This pretty Christmas swag was constructed on a wire frame covered with moss. First, a green satin wired bow was fixed at the top of the frame so that the plant material would cover part of it and prevent it from appearing too dominant. Then I wired in a dried protea (*Protea*) at the bottom for a tassel effect. I wired some gold plastic leaves, fixing one at the top and widening the centre of the swag with several more. I ran these leaves towards the base to create just the right outline. The two plastic peppers were a good size, shape and texture but needed livening up a little so they were sprayed gold. The three waxed lilies (*Lilium*) were a dirty white when I bought them from a street market so these were sprayed gold too, along with some equally tatty roses (*Rosa*). When they had been sprayed, wired and fixed in position their transformation was complete. Three bunches of green artificial grapes down the left side of the swag and a bunch of gold grapes on the right side at the top for balance provided the finishing touches.

Facing page: An elegant Christmas swag

christmas topiary tree

Facing page: A topiary tree in bright Christmas colours

This attractive topiary tree in bright Christmas colours is simple and economical to make. The container used here is plastic, and a good colour and style for a topiary tree, but it did need a heavy weight in the base to keep it balanced.

Having constructed the basic tree (see page 44), I cut two branches of silk variegated holly into small sprays, wired them and placed them around the tree, turning it as I worked to achieve the right shape. Then several more small pieces of holly were put at the base of the Oasis so that the finished tree would not look completely round. I wired in pine cones, some of them gilded, and gold baubles around the Oasis. Next I positioned the wired red ribbon roses and the fairly large red berries. Several small bunches of gold grapes were positioned carefully to provide a contrast in texture. Two ribbon bows of the same red as the roses were wired lower down on each side of the stem. This provided a stronger link between the container and the tree, helping to balance the whole arrangement. Finally, I put reindeer moss at the top of the container.

individual arrangements

royal worcester plate

Antique patterned plates are used mainly for display purposes and are becoming rather rare. However, plates with patterned borders are still readily available – probably because people tend to prefer decorative centres. Here I decided to create a floral decoration for the centre of one of my dinner plates.

To prepare the plate for the arrangement, I first cut across one-third of a small cylindrical brown Oasis and slope-cut around its top edge. The Oasis was then glued to the plate with Copydex and left with a weight on top until completely firm (at least four hours). I chose green, gold and cream as the colour scheme and took shapes and textures into account while selecting the plant material; the aim was to achieve a balance between the ornate border and the arrangement itself. These plates look best on a stand or hung on a wall – but don't forget to blow the dust away occasionally!

The two gold fern-like leaves were positioned first, overlapping the rim slightly at the top of the plate. I then worked leaves – green silk, gold silk and gold filigree – down each side, leaving a small space at the bottom for a gold ribbon bow and a narrow green one just above it. Ribbon roses of the same colour as the green ribbon bow were positioned next, followed by a balance of flowers, gilded cones, artificial berries and baubles. The largest cream, artificial, star-shaped flower was placed at the focal point. To complete the arrangement, I cut small stalks of dried grass to varying lengths, pointed one end of each and inserted them underneath the ribbon bows.

Facing page: This pretty spray livens up the otherwise plain centre of this attractive dinner plate

antique porcelain bowl

Facing page: It is the bunches of grapes falling over the front of this lovely bowl that give the whole arrangement a sensuous appearance

This figure bowl was cracked when I bought it, otherwise it would have been too expensive to use for flowers! It is a lovely piece, although not the easiest choice for an arrangement. White is obviously the dominant colour and it was therefore necessary to include white flowers within the actual arrangement. I prepared the container by cutting a piece of brown Oasis to fit tightly in the base of the bowl, leaving 2.5cm (1in) above the rim.

The well-wired, rich, dark-maroon grapes were positioned first to tumble over the sides. These provided a strong contrast with the white of the container. I had managed to find some artificial fruit and rosehips of a similar colour and positioned these next. Then I added some white silk roses (*Rosa*) and, to complete the arrange-ment, I put in a few white silk freesias (*Freesia*) and some wired glycerined dark-coloured leaves to pick up the colour of the fruits.

pewter mug

The neutral colour of pewter blends well with flowers, dried material in particular. For this arrangement, I used a few pieces of wired glycerined conifer and heather (*Erica*) in the body of the arrangement, draping some over at the front, and placed appropriately sized glycerined leaves in the centre. The arrangement began to take on a country look, which I decided I would develop further.

I put in various shades of small wired strawflowers (*Helichrysum*) for colour and the globe amaranth (*Gomphrena globosa*) and safflowers (*Carthamus*) provided more solid shapes. I separated some pale-lemon achillea (*Achillea*) into small sprays, wiring and inserting these at the sides. Next I added the small poppy (*Papaver*) seedheads for their colour and texture. Finally, I placed a ribbon bow just above the handle, not so much to fill a space as to tone with the other reds and pinks.

Above and facing page: The brightly-coloured strawflowers really bring this pretty, but simple-to-make, arrangement to life

victorian steel urn

Facing page: A striking arrangement made with light- and dark-pink dried and silk flowers

The shape of the urn dictated the style of this arrangement. In preparation, I fixed a round cylindrical Oasis almost level with the top of the container so the plant material could be positioned to continue the line of the urn.

The dried and silk delphiniums (*Delphinium*) followed the shape of the urn upwards, creating the height and the outline. Dried and silk roses (*Rosa*), both dark and light pink, provided depth and intensity of colour while the strawflowers (*Helichrysum*) added a new texture. Finally, I inserted some silk leaves chosen for their subtle colours – they can look most unnatural if they are too bright.

Tip: View the arrangement from every angle when applying the finishing touches.

posy on marble base

After a great deal of thought as to the best way to use this marble base, I decided on a posy arrangement with a pale colour scheme. I put a round brown cylindrical Oasis in a plastic saucer and fixed this into the bowl of the marble base with three pieces of Oasis fix.

I used plastic ferns, leaves and fruit to establish the shades of cream and brown. I positioned the wired fawn-coloured ferns first to form the background. Their pale, 'lacy' appearance suited the marble base particularly well. I removed and wired individual orange/brown fruits and leaves from bunches, using them to introduce a slightly bolder colour, and positioned the cream slub satin ribbon roses in strategic places for a smooth texture. I wanted to echo the faint blue/grey veins running through the marble base in the arrangement itself and chose pale-blue silk hydrangeas (*Hydrangea*) for this purpose. I wired the hydrangea florets separately before placing them in the Oasis, and heightened their colour with the small, round, blue-grey fruits.

Facing page: A delicate arrangement for an unusual marble stand

cabbage dish

I decided that the texture and shape of this unusual dark-green cabbage dish would be ideal for a small bouquet-style arrangement. The first step was to prepare the dish for use, which I did by cutting a brown cylindrical Oasis in half and gluing it to the bottom of the dish. It is equally possible to secure Oasis on a plastic prong attached to a container with Oasis fix.

I began by placing the bunch of wired black grapes at the front of the dish and then put in the pink silk flowers, leaving a space for the two pomegranates in the foreground. Next I inserted a few green leaves and black cherries and finally, a wired chiffon-patterned ribbon bow, which picked up on all the shades of the flowers and fruits.

Right: A pot-pourri of pinkish fruits and flowers

sunflowers

Facing page: A simple but bright and cheerful arrangement made from sunflowers and twisted bamboo sticks

These were some of the most attractive silk sunflowers (*Helianthus*) I had ever seen and I could not resist buying them. They needed placing in a fairly simple container which would allow their bold shape and cheerful yellow to dominate. I eventually chose a grey/brown clay pot which I felt was just the right size, colour and texture and cut a piece of brown Oasis to fit across the middle.

I positioned the sunflowers first, leaving the leaves on the stems, and then wired some extra leaves (which were similar in appearance to the sunflowers'), together with some fairly large glycerined leaves to boost the foliage. I then added several twisted bamboo sticks (available from florists and garden centres) which provided an interesting contrast in shape as well as complementing the colour of the container.

dome lidded box

This box has a lovely lid and the mellow tones of the lining make it most suitable for a floral display. The lid also has a brass fixture which allows it to stay secured at any angle.

I had bought the two large pink silk flowers some time before I found the box, hoping that they would come in useful one day and was delighted when they seemed to fit so perfectly into place within this arrangement! I positioned them first, in order to establish the proportions and the choice of colours for the rest of the arrangement. The wired peach and pomegranates continued the delicate pink tones, while the four large proteas (*Protea*) and some medium-sized pine cones provided textural contrast. I then fixed in the wired grape-type berries to look as though they were spilling from the front of the box. Green foliage would not have been at all suitable, so I used glycerined beech (*Fagus sylvatica*) and mahonia (*Mahonia*) branches as their copper tones matched the box beautifully. Finally, I put in some box (*Buxus*) stems, which had turned a lovely pale brown.

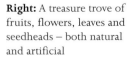

Right: A treasure trove of fruits, flowers, leaves and seedheads – both natural and artificial

bird scene

Slices of wood such as the base used for this arrangement are sold at florists. They are varnished on one side and left natural on the other – both sides are useful.

For this scene, I glued a small rectangular piece of brown Oasis to the rough side of the wood slice, just off centre. I cut each of the four small contorted willow (*Salix matsudana* 'Tortuosa') branches to a point at one end and inserted them into the Oasis, applying glue to fix them securely in place. Then I glued moss sparingly on to the Oasis and the wood, leaving spaces for small rocks and stones (and for some of the wood to show through) around the perimeter. Next I included small clusters of silk snowdrops *(Galanthus nivalis)* and daisies, a sprig of dried heather (*Erica*) and three artificial mushrooms. The finishing touch was provided by wiring the artificial birds on to two branches.

Facing page: An unusual but dramatic bird scene arrangement

art nouveau figure

Facing page: Containers and stands of different sizes and shapes can be used for flower arrangements. This graceful art nouveau figure provides the perfect basis for a sophisticated, flowing arrangement

This stand presented me with a real challenge! It was a daunting job to ensure that the arrangement followed the same graceful lines established by the stand itself, but I found a wired spray of velvet leaves which I thought would help to create a light, 'floating' sense of movement.

First of all, I glued a brown cylindrical Oasis firmly into the bowl held by the figure, leaving 2.5cm (1in) above the rim. I then inserted the wired spray of velvet leaves into the Oasis on the right so that it extended in a flowing line over the edge of the bowl. This was the really essential piece of material and therefore had to be securely fixed in the right position. Next I wired some more velvet leaves separately and placed them at different angles through the arrangement right around the bowl. There were some small green details both on the figure and on the bowl, so I put in five slender leaves of a similar delicate green, two at the left and right and one in the centre. I also added some cream and pale-lemon paper roses (*Rosa*). The colours of the two different sprays of berries, together with the covered wire tendrils, helped to complete the picture. The arrangement required a base for balance, and the oval chipboard covered with mauve Dralon was just right.

modern chinese fish tank

Facing page: If you use a patterned container such as this, choose a fairly bright colour scheme but do not use too many different types of material or the finished arrangement will look too fussy

Any large, attractive container can be used for an arrangement such as this. It is really not as difficult as it looks to create a beautiful and original design. I often put some pieces of crumpled newspaper in the bottom of a large, opaque container as it means there is less space to fill and it also helps to prevent any potential movement of the material.

For this arrangement, I inserted three silk leaf plants opened out though still all wired together. These provided a background and helped to anchor the rest of the material. The silk roses (*Rosa*) had the most realistic leaves and their pretty, delicate stamens made them even more attractive. Lady's mantle (*Alchemilla mollis*), asparagus fern and lamb's tongue (*Stachys lanata*) were growing in my garden, ready to be picked for drying, so I decided to experiment and find out if they would dry in situ. I added them to the arrangement and left them for a few days. The lady's mantle and the asparagus fern dried satisfactorily but the lamb's tongue went limp so I transferred it to a warm airing cupboard for four days, after which it was fully dried and once again took its place in the arrangement. This little experiment proved just how easily such plants can be dried.

mixed posy

Posies have many different uses. They can be displayed on a side table, hung on a wall to brighten up a blank space or used to decorate a dinner plate at the beginning of a celebratory meal. A posy can be pinned to a dress or jacket for a special occasion or, for a stylishly wrapped present, try fixing one to the top of a plain gift box. This attractive little posy is made up of silk, dried and glycerined material, as well as a paper rose, artificial fruit and a ribbon rose and bow – all wired and stem taped. It illustrates just how well most of the materials featured in this book go together.

Left and facing page:
Mixed posy

useful addresses

Antique containers
Barnsdale Antique Centre
The Avenue
Rutland Water (Nr Oakham)
Leics LE1 8AH
Tel: 01572 722322

Flowers, fruit and sundries
Dried Flower Inspirations
The Midlands Floral Warehouse
12-20 Kingsley Street
Leics LE2 6DL
Tel: 0116 2706019

Florist wholesalers
Bantock Flowers Ltd
Unit 8
Weldon Road
Loughborough
Leics LE11 0RN
Tel: 01509 232992

Unusual fresh and dried flowers
Fleur de Lys
Haven House
Springbridge Road
Ealing
London W5 2AA
Tel: 01509 232992

Dried flowers
The Hop Shop
Castle Farm
Shoreham
Sevenoaks
Kent TN14 7UB
Tel: 01959 523219

Dried and artificial flowers, sundries
The Diddybox
132-134 Belmont Road
Bolton
Lancs BL1 7AN
Tel: 01204 595610

Baskets and containers
Joanna Wood Ltd
48a Pimlico Road
London SW1W 8LP
Tel: 0171 730 4135

Dried flowers and sundries
Everlasting Garden
89 George Street
Hove
Sussex
Tel: 01273 777504

Dried flowers
Cottage Flowers
The Cottage
114 Thorkhill Road
Thames Ditton
Surrey KT7 0UW
Tel: 0181 224 0124

Dried and artificial flowers, sundries
John Lewis
Oxford Street
London W1A 1EX
Tel: 0171 6297711

Florists' sundries
Whichcraft Workshops
Park Farm Oast
Maresfield
East Sussex TN22 2EE
Tel: 01273 777504

further reading

FARJON, Mireille
Dried Flowers for the Home
B.T. Batsford Ltd, London (1993)

HAMILTON, Anne and WHITE, Kathleen
Making Silk Flowers
Merehurst, London (1993)

HILLIER, Malcolm
Pocket Encyclopedia of Flower Arranging
Dorling Kindersley, London (1990)

HILLIER, Malcolm and HILTON, Colin
The Complete Book of Dried Flowers
Dorling Kindersely, London (1986)

LAWRENCE, Mary
Dried Flowers
Salamander Books Ltd, London (1987)

LAWRENCE, Mary and WATERKEYN, Sarah
Dried and Pressed Flowers
Salamander Books Ltd, London (1988)

RADCLIFFE, Barbara Rogers
Drying Flowers
Merehurst Ltd, London (1992)

RAWORTH, Jenny and BERRY, Susan
The Dried Flower Arranger's Year
Collins & Brown, London (1993)

SHEEN, Joanna
The Dried Flower Project Book
Merehurst, London (1994)

VAGG, Daphne
The Flower Arrangers A-Z
B.T. Batsford Ltd, London (1989)

WESTLAND, Pamela
Decorating with Dried Flowers
Quintet Publishing Ltd, London (1991)

WOODHAMS, Stephen
The Country Dried Flower Companion
Mitchell Beazley, London (1995)

index